BREAK HEARTS WITHOUT MERCY

How to break up and heal fast

Sonia Vela

Copyright

DISCLAIMER

I have tried to be as accurate and complete as possible in creating this report, although you do not have support or a view at any time that the contents are accurate due to the rapid change of the Internet.

While I have made every effort to verify the information provided in this publication, I assume no responsibility for errors, omissions, or misinterpretations. Any mentions of specific people, persons, or organizations are unintentional.

I do not intend this document for use as a source of legal, business, accounting, or financial advice. I advise all readers to find the services of professionals who have expertise in the law, money, accounting, and finance field.

I encourage you to print this book for easy reading.

Table of Contents

Wrapping it up

20 reasons why you should move on and without him.

Introduction

Separation in relationships can be a very difficult process, especially if the relationship was important. Being happy with our lives is important to us, and if your partner isn't making you happy, maybe it's time to move on. Below are some tips to end a relationship.

BREAK HEARTS WITHOUT MERCY

How to break up and heal fast.

Chapter One

Introduction

Do you want to end your relationship with your lover or husband? If so, you must know the rules of ending a relationship. Believe it or not, there are some rules about how to end a relationship.

If you have been with your husband or boyfriend for a long time, it is important to be careful. You cannot send a notification and SMS to them that it is over. This is the worst way to break up - even if you've been with them for 2-5 years.

Having been with someone for a long time, they may have many feelings for you. Remember that time creates precious memories for others and if you are ready to move on, it may not be the same for him or her.

This is exactly why you should break up slowly. After a divorce, some people will experience great emotions, such as anxiety, depression, and even anger. Always respect other people's feelings and don't play with them. Always make your separations in private if you want to avoid drama. You never know if your partner will scream or cry. If they have a strong relationship with you, you will not be able to avoid breaking their heart.

People can be very emotional. Without relationships, we would not be able to rebuild or move forward in our lives.

Now, before you explode, you have to think about why you want to leave the relationship. You should know the answer by now. You can move on because your partner treated you badly.

or

Because he fell in love with someone else. Another example is newlyweds. In this case, you are not testing the waters to find your true match. Don't deny yourself happiness by holding back. Breaking up with your partner can be a painful experience, but in the next few months, you will start to forget about it.

For some people, it can take years to improve. This is because when dating, there are people who always compare other people to their exes. This is not advisable.

Moving on is not a good idea and you will not be able to enjoy your new relationship if you are still thinking about your ex.

Chapter Two

How to end a relationship

To end a relationship, you must first think about what you will say to your partner. At least they deserve it. Also note why you want to break up.

Tell them you will miss them and say it with love when you speak. The worst way to break up is to yell or argue. Remember that you still have to be strong. Otherwise, they may tell you that they will not accept a divorce.

Practical advice

Here are some tips for you:

Speak calmly when explaining the reasons. Do you want to make sure that your partner understands everything?

Watch your partner as you speak and be firm to let them know you mean it. Meet them in person at a supermarket, restaurant, or cafe. He will assess the situation if they decide to be angry.

Let them know how much you care about them and that they will continue to be mean a lot to you. Expressing feelings is a good way to avoid conflict.

Tell them what you love about the relationship and get into the problems of a relationship.

By doing so, you not only show his bad qualities but also the good things you see in him.

Then tell him about being friends or having no contact at all. You have to accept it. This is called maintaining social boundaries without anyone interfering in your life.

Talk about details when it comes to spending time with friends and family members. Decide on two other candidates to share.

If they try to start a fight, watch out. However, if things get worse, let them know it will go away. Tell them you don't want to fight or cause a situation. Hopefully, they will understand and calm down before you go.

These are some useful techniques for washing. Since you will be around many people, it is less likely that the situation will explode in front of you or cause an argument. Do not bring friends or family because you will embarrass the other person you are dating.

Chapter Three

Evidence of a Bad Relationship

In some relationships, persuasion, manipulation, and promises are tools employed by people. If you are with someone who is like this, breaking up will not be easy.

Don't Be Foolish

They will probably approach you and tell you that everything will change back to the way things were before. It may even seem that they are honest, with their bad behavior fading away. Remember that this is all action and most people will not change unless they are your true love. I do believe that they behave in the same way with their friends and only put up that for you; it is a good sign that they are not interested in change.

Some breakups are so devastating to the other person that they feel like they can't move on

In life. Their emotions start to spiral and they are a mess. Without you In their life, they feel lost without it. With such a precedent, you need to take the matter seriously. If they are used to mentioning suicides, always take them seriously. Keep chatting with them in words while calling the police.

These people are very fragile when it comes to relationships. If they have been faking it, your ex will quickly learn the consequences by not doing this again. Once the police are called, they will take your ex to the nearest mental hospital, which is also used for suicide prevention. The safety of your ex should make you feel better.

In these types of places, they will bring an individual into a room with only a bed. There are no hard objects in the room that can be utilized for their suicide activities. There are also cameras in the room, with a live person monitoring them 24/7. They can make people be there for it 24 hours or a week. Counseling sessions are available if your ex needs to talk to somebody.

Most of the time, you will not be able to move on since you have built up a fear deep inside. You often worry about what your ex might say or do to your friends to get you back. If you are in this situation, you will need to take risks. If they plan to do something illegal, make sure you notify the authorities. These types of people are pathetic at best and the best thing to do is avoid them completely. This means changing your phone number, changing job positions, and even transferring to another school. They obviously cannot blackmail you if there is no contact. Be sure to tell family members not to make calls to your ex.

Here are some evidence of a bad relationship. These signs will help you get out quickly:

Anger

By picking up the warning signs of anger in a man, you will stop yourself from entering into an abusive relationship. Angry men tend to hold your arm, forces you to do things you don't want to, and even push you to take action with something you don't want to have anything to do with. You might think this is part of them, but you don't know.

Blackmail

Most of the time, depression can lead to low self-esteem. Maybe when you and your ex were intimate, and he took some pictures showing his underwear. He said if you leave, he will send these to every girl he knows. Someone you love,

you will care about his emotions, even if they can't be with you.

Low self-esteem

Being in a relationship that is froth with physical or mental problems can make a hole in your heart, causing your body to shrink. Instead of being the fun, happy person you used to be - you seem to be walking around with your shoulders down. You don't enjoy the things you used to do and this low self-esteem will eventually lead to depression.

Manipulation

Did you know that manipulation is the number #1 reason why men and women stop going out together? For example, if you tell your lady that you want to leave her because of her bad habits, you will manipulate her just by making them feel guilty. The sad puppy eyes turned over and tears began to roll down her cheeks. He says he will die without you and you fear he will do something stupid like killing himself.

Instead, get him help right away and go slowly. Don’t tell him directly that you are moving on, but just take some time to distance yourself from him.

Mental Abuse

Being mentally abused is never fun. Mental abuse often starts with name-calling, being ridiculed, and even being embarrassed in front of others. Sometimes, these name-calling could be in front of friends. He wants to appear masculine and in control. In reality, this is not a person who respects your feelings, and the mental abuse will only get worse. Get out while you still can!

Physical Abuse

Both men and women can be sexual towards each other. It doesn’t just go for men.

Many women beat their husbands in anger. It is physical abuse. It is important and if you are abused, move away. If you have injuries from abuse, it is important to contact your local law enforcement. Don’t let them treat you like this. There are many good men and women out there who will give you the respect and dignity you deserve.

Chapter Four

Tips for Ending a Relationship Without Stress

The breakup process is not easy these days unless you stick to a phone call or text. Don't have a friend over and don't write about it. These are some of the worst breakups we've ever seen. Make sure you set a date to see your boyfriend or girlfriend but don't give them any idea that you are breaking up with them, otherwise they might not want to give up.

Do It The Right Way

Here are tips on what to do when you break up:

Do not try to separate by a letter or text.

Don't let your partner know you plan on breaking up before you set a date.

Don't be shy or raise your voice during the break.

Avoid breaking through a letter.

Don't tell friends you're breaking up until you tell your partner first. When you break up, do it

don't do it in front of other people you know well.

Do not create an official announcement that you are separated.

These are the worst ways to break up and if you want to keep a friendship between the two of you, it's better to respect that person. This will allow you to have a healthy friendship with them and avoid events that can lead to stress. Let's be realistic- breaking up is not an event to look forward to.

Feelings that someone has never had before can often surface and it's easy to explode when you see the girl or man of your dreams leaving you. You will always feel deserted, sad, and lost.

Also, know that some people can't be friends after a breakup. If you miss your girlfriend and she doesn't want to be friends, you should accept this. The reality of it is not being with him might just be too much pain for him to take. Over time, there is a chance that it can get better. As you spend more time with friends, start working on your homework, books, and enjoy life without him- there is a good chance that he can come back.

Now, we mean to come back as a friend and not a boyfriend or husbands. Let's switch sides here.

What if your ex-boyfriend from six months ago contacted you on Facebook? Please don't think he wants to get back together. Instead, know that he still cares for you and you just want to know how you are doing. He does not know if you are seeing someone, are living in another country, or already have a family. Make sure you have an open mind and don't think.

Chapter Five

Options For Changes, Counseling, And Guidance

Every day, hundreds of people break up for the wrong reasons. For example - you might be with a wonderful person who cares for you deeply but doesn't show it through talking.

You have noticed that you are this way with everyone- especially family members. Even though you guys have been together for 4 months, you still don't talk much. However, this man is getting ready to decide for you because he is madly in love with you. Love someone because they are called infinite love. If you have a kind heart and always take care of yourself well, you should think twice about breaking up. Here are some examples of changes between relationships, guidance, and counseling.

Patch Things Up

Before we go on some of the events that may occur, let's talk about the importance of counseling. By seeing a relationship adviser every week, you will be able to let out sadness without arguments. This is a safe way of discussing everything in a civilized way. A counselor is there to record your progress and also make sure that you are not dragged into a big argument, which is what happens many times as well

in couples. Many times, a man or woman will not speak out because they are afraid of what other people will think, which in this case, is bullying.

What about breaking up to chase another person? This is the worst idea even though many people have done it. Your lover is someone who works a lot and you go through the stress of being a stay-at-home mom who does everything before he gets home. He is unbelievably sweet and outgoing. By the time he gets home, he turns into a different person. He is shouting at you and tells you that you need to contribute more.

Now, you have talked with your friend who has been working with you before. He is your friend, amazingly handsome and smart. You have always wanted to see where things can develop, so you are thinking of ending the relationship with your fiancée.

The same situation can happen with the new guy you want, especially if there is a special relationship to happen.

Chapter Six

Test Relationship Solutions

Even if you were the one to initiate the breakup, moving on can be overwhelming even to you. Also, it's normal to feel sad about the breakup and you find yourself sometimes trying to stop yourself from texting or calling your ex. Let's say you broke up because of their bad behavior Your boyfriend is always late, always smokes, and swears at your family. You have tried to change his habits because you think you can change him. As sad as it might sound, the truth is the changes you look forward to seeing in him might not happen.

A few tested relative solutions recommended before moving on are listed

below. Make sure you go over everything carefully because this could be your ticket to saving relationships:

Speech

Before going further, you need to have "the word". Let him know the direction you are heading to and make sure to let him know how important this is to you. Talking allows you to let out your frustrations and gratitude in a relationship. Tell them what behaviors you don't approve of and ask how they can change for you.

The promises

If you both know you are in an unhealthy relationship, why not promise each other? For example, if your boyfriend disrespects you by calling you names out of anger, make him promise not to do this again. He will ask you to stop making fun of him in front of your friends and this will be your promise. Having a rule or boundaries between you two is a big help.

Love

Do you feel like you are falling out of love with the person you are with? If so, you might want to recreate the magic and see what you can do to keep it as it were before when the two met. Why don't you bring back old memories and go to a restaurant with the two of you? Serious. Light candles or bring flowers if you like. This will get the sparks flying again!

Moving on is not something you can do within a few days. It takes months or even years to agree on a significant one who loves you, even if the breakup was your idea.

being trapped in a relationship that is not happy will just make you want to escape. If you've tried everything and there are no more options, it's a dead end. Remember that it is not the end of the world. You will probably meet someone new.

To continue, you will need to push yourself into new activities. Go out more with your girlfriends. Girls' night is always a great way to please yourself, even if you can't stop thinking about your ex.

Why not put in more extra hours for work? You can earn some extra money and break up with your ex. However, if he works in the same field as you, you will probably look at other job opportunities.

The hardest time is at night. Your heart and mind will be confused, thinking memories. This is when you feel the need to call or text them. Rather than being sad and let all your emotions roll in, pick up a good book. By reading each night, you will stop worrying about other people and you will be able to focus on your own needs.

If you still have trouble moving forward, it's a good idea to seek help from others. Through communication skills, you will be able to identify what bothers you the most. If you don't have friends to talk to or just feel uncomfortable, you can opt for mental counseling. A psychiatrist is there to listen to your feelings and sometimes give advice on what to do. Your progress will be monitored and any noticeable positive changes will be communicated to you. Also, when you get advice always keep a diary with you. As time goes by, you will not be as fixated on your ex as you were before.

Chapter Seven

How to Respond to Good and Bad Advice on Ending a Relationship Including the One You Are Reading Now.

To respond to good and bad advice on ending a relationship, you need to be confident and know everything that is happening around you. Communication is also a factor when it comes to ending the relationship. Make sure you focus on these three things I will explain later.

However, when people tell you to stick with a terrible relationship, you can get terrible and this is wrong. Men and women often leave a relationship when they realize that it is no longer good for their mental and physical health.

Taking Advice

Now, here are some tips for when deciding whether to end a relationship.

Trust

Having confidence that you can continue is very important. You probably feel like you cannot love anyone else at this point, but this is not true. Time will slowly begin to heal you, allowing room for new relationships to develop.

Instead of sulking in your room, get out of the house. Go ahead and join community activities as a volunteer.

This is a great way to open up to other people and take your mind off things. There are many volunteer events, such as gardening, garbage collection, joining the health center, and helping children in need. With confidence, you will be sure that you will recover in a short amount of time. You just need to have faith in yourself.

Knowledge

Being aware of your feelings is your first step to progress. Stop holding back on your emotions. It's okay to cry now and then. If you don't let your feelings out, you may still feel sad. It will prevent you from moving on and taking control of your life. If you have a hard time realizing your feelings, music will often help. Listen to music that has lyrics that express deep emotion. You will start to have the same emotions, too.

Communication

Being able to communicate with others will not only make you feel better, but you will also be able to move beyond this situation. By talking with others, you get to free up your clogged mind. What must you do to release any feelings you have? You can open up and talk to your friends and or family members about the situation. They will give you advice or just be that person who will listen.

Normally, when we are acknowledged in life by others, it will open a door. The path that passes through this gate leads to peace, happiness, and harmony.

Chapter Eight

Benefits of Satisfaction In a Relationship

If you're not sure about moving forward, it's probably not a good idea to break up in the first place. You need to decide if the relationship is strong and worth saving.

There are many benefits of satisfaction within the relationship and by moving on, you can't learn about these benefits. Here are some tips on how to get everything together and find the source of why all of your issues persist.

The person you are with can be good for you, but you will need help first. Change is always possible, but you cannot do this with force. Encouraging your partner positively for change is on of the best ways to overcome relationship problems. This can also help develop good habits for partner.

Talking to your other half about any problems in the relationship is important when it comes to finding a solution. If they seem hesitant or not ready for changes, you should consider moving on. However, if they show signs of change, it is advisable give them another chance.

Although, in the future, they may return to their old ways and once this happens, it's time to call it quits. You should be with someone who cares for you that they will marry to change their habits. Making sacrifices is what love is all about.

Go through everything that you both are having problems with. It may not be for one important problem. Many times, divorce results because of many small issues that are often brought up.

Both of you may be angry with each other and take revenge. This is not healthy for the relationship. To start making changes, tell your husband what's bothering you.

Don't accuse them or yell at them when you start talking about problems. Praise them for what they have done today and move on to the next topic. By expressing your feelings when they do something specific, you can even make them feel guilty. Making them guilty is not the goal, but it can still be effective. Your partner will know your sensitivity and can even apologize, looking for an answer on how to fix the problem.

Remember, it's not what you say, but how you present the subject yourself.

Chapter Nine

Merits Of Moving On Without Your Significant Other After A Long Time

Moving forward without your partner can make you a stronger person in the future. Although moving out can be one of the most difficult things in your life, you will benefit from this move. If you are with someone angry, he doesn't care about your feelings, and he is selfish - this person is not someone you would want to be with.

The best thing about moving on is that you will not have him emotionally drag you to the floor. If you are around someone who treats you badly, you will lose confidence in yourself. Surround yourself with positive people while moving forward. You can speak out with a few girlfriends to boost your spirits. I'm sure they've gone through the situation the same size and can give you a helping hand. By living with your ex, you may even become depressed.

For example, if your boyfriend has been unfaithful to you three times throughout the relationship, this will bring you down. You will probably think something is not right with you. Am I pretty enough for him? The problem is not with you.

Some men are simply not ready to settle down and change their habits. If they are young, this is very true.

Now, this does not mean going out another day with men, heck NO. Instead, focus on yourself. How can you develop good habits and change yourself as a pers? By doing things like going to school, showing up for work each day, and even volunteering in activities - you will be able to meet people who are interested in the same things as you. It is a good idea to meet women, but if you have a few male friends along the way, this is good too. Develop some friendships instead of dating. You may be ready to date again in the future, and who knows? The people you like may even be waiting for this.

Wrapping it up

20 Reasons To Break Up With A Toxic Partner.

There are many reasons why you should continue without the relationship. You may be delayed. You come down in life to do things you would not like to do or even prevent you from meeting a person who is good for you. It doesn't matter if you are a young woman or an old woman There is plenty of life ahead of us to see what is there. A lot of good can happen in your life in such a little time that you will be impressed.

Remember that sometimes we will move forward for a reason. Even if you don't think so and move on from your boyfriend, it will be better. Time always heals the mind.

You might miss him and feel like you cannot do without him, but you will eventually meet someone else. By meeting someone else that is good for you and treats you well, you will then know there are good men out there. They are hard to find, but if you start hanging out with people who have good habits, you will set yourself up for praise.

Here are 20 reasons why you should move on and without him.

1. To have new experiences and improve things in your life.

2. Live life to the fullest without letting it get you down.

3. Enjoy your friends more.

4. Get to know yourself.

5. Focus on your work.

6. Focus on your studies.

7. Reform your family life and build stronger family bonds.

8. Being free from harassment and abuse.

9. Being free from someone who doesn't want you.

10. Be able to meet other guys who are good for you.

11. Develop a strong relationship with your (spiritual) body.

12. Begin to seek help from God.

13. Taking your health seriously, especially your mental health.

14. Surround yourself with good people.

15. Be able to recognize your emotions.

16. Do not lead a manipulative lifestyle

17. Stay away from the man who has no respect for you.

18. Take control of your life goals.

19. Being able to concentrate on your work.

20. Establish a safe zone for yourself.

Best regards.

Sonia Vela

www.ingramcontent.com/pod-product-compliance
Lightning Source LLC
LaVergne TN
LVHW020543160826
845677LV00015B/4172

* 9 7 9 8 8 4 4 3 0 8 5 1 2 *